Have I Finally Found Out How To Just "Be"?

ONE MAN'S JOURNEY
FROM MARITAL CRISIS TO SELF-DISCOVERY

Have I Finally Found Out How To Just "Be"?

ONE MAN'S JOURNEY
FROM MARITAL CRISIS TO SELF-DISCOVERY

EDITED BY PAT GAUDETTE

Home & Leisure Publishing, Inc.

Have I Finally Found Out How To Just "Be"?
One Man's Journey from Marital Crisis to Self-Discovery

Published by
Home & Leisure Publishing, Inc.
P O Box 968
Lecanto, Florida 34460
www.halpi.com

Copyright 2012 Pat Gaudette

ISBN 978-0-9847852-0-9 (paperback)
ISBN 978-0-9847852-1-6 (e-book)

Library of Congress Control Number: 2012903071

Cover image © 2012 Jupiterimages Corporation

Printed in the United States of America

It's at the borders of pain and suffering that the men are separated from the boys. ~ Emil Zatopek

The following is a journal of self-discovery by a man I will refer to as "John." His journal covers a span of 89 days during which he struggles to come to grps with his wife's betrayal and subsequent exit from their marriage, their impending divorce, and his new role as a middle-aged single parent.

While "John" is not his real name, he *is* a real person struggling with issues that many men (and women) will be able to relate to. These are his words, edited to provide anonymity for all parties involved.

~ Pat Gaudette

Day 1

There are clouds in my life right now. That is for sure. I have an appointment tomorrow morning with orthopedic doctor. It was painful today every time I had to move. I stayed home but work called several times about the project and telling me the clock is ticking.

So I will do whatever it takes to get this job done. The people I work with are wonderful. I couldn't have picked another bunch of people to work with. I just feel lately, I have been letting them down.

I have a girl that is coming over this weekend and says don't worry I will help with the house and get the kids going on helping too.

I mentioned to my wife this morning about my knee and such. All she said is that she will go to the school and drop off our littlest son's backpack she had in her car since Saturday. No calls. No visits. No nothing. She is just building up more hatred towards her.

The kids helped me some but didn't clean up. That hurt a little bit too.

The sun... it shines every day in my life right now. It's just that I have to go and find it. It doesn't come to me right now like it used to.

Day 2

One does have to take care of one's self. I found that out this evening. I collapsed, almost passed out while doing dishes. I hobbled to the bedroom, closed the door and cried.

I must back up here. I went to the doctor today. Got X-rays of the knee. All looked good as far as any deformities or breakage. No swelling. They set me up for an MRI that will give more detail of the cartilage and tendons. From that they will know more of what is going on.

No meds were given. I went to work and came home at the end of the day.

I got home and my kids naturally were in full bore. We couldn't eat because no dishes to eat off of. I got a call from the wife asking me to take the two oldest ones tomorrow night at around 8 or 9 and drop them off at her work.

She asked how's it going? I said my knee gave out and I can't get around. It's really hurting. She said sorry. Said goodbye. We hung up.

I proceeded to go wash the dishes and while washing them everything seemed to come to a head. Emotionally and physically. The room swirled and I found myself on my knees with the sponge and a platter in my hands. My oldest put his arm around me and said, Daddy are you OK? I put up the front and stood up and composed myself and said I'm OK.

That's when I went to my room and shut the door and cried my eyes out. That hasn't happened in many many months.

I am in a somber state right now. To where I don't give a crap about anything. NO! No! No! I can't do that!!! I have to keep it up. Have to keep my life going so the kids can be happy.

I am a giving person overboard. That's not bad when everything is ok but now I have to be a person that gives to myself. This is the mirror that I saw this evening.

I feel I have been used by life, by other people taking advantage of my good will. Ah! A fork in the road here.

There it goes again. Cryptic. I don't seem to explain it any other way sometimes without metaphors. Because I am trying to write the unexplainable feelings one has. I guess.

Maybe I think, I will let everything "BE." Try that for awhile. Cynical. Am I getting cynical in life? I'll have to look that word up in the dictionary.

This was my day and I always have seen the glass half full in my life. And still do.

Day 3

I have to work Saturday and Sunday. My project at work is coming due. It's going good but requires the hours to finish it.

I have and my wife has in the past done all the things for our sons. I thought we were teaching them to have life skills. They do. But they are lazy. And complain and balk so much that it tires me out and I cave in.

Now that I know that and actually knew that, I will not cave in. Nor will I stand there and argue. No work. No play! It takes at least 21 to 30 days consistency to make it into a routine, a habit. I have let them run over me too long.

I called the wife and said I have to work this weekend. She said, do you have a sitter? Or do I have to do it. I said I can get a sitter. She immediately said no. Just take the two youngest ones over my apartment in the morning and after we get around noon we will go to the park and take them out.

I didn't want that. I said can't you sit with them at the house? She sighed and said no. That it will be a nice day and that they need to get outside.

I then said well I wanted them to do some cleaning of the house that they need to do. She said that after their day out, she will take them to the house to clean. I know how that will be. Minimal if not nothing.

I do have this girl that will come over and stay for the weekend and stay with the kids. I don't know whether to call up the wife and say no. I have someone else. She doesn't seem to care about our house and the condition it's in. I should just say that the boys have to come home and do all their chores and then they can go out with you (mommy).

My knee feels somewhat better today. I took Ibuprofen. 400mg. It is less stiff today than it was yesterday so that's a good sign.

Well it's back to work.

Day 4

It's been a busy Saturday with me working on my project at work. It went well and on schedule.

Which bridge to burn and which bridge to walk on. That is what has ended my night with. Vince Gill. Oh how he has good words.

I have been drinking tequila and beer chasers.

While I was away my wife and the girl that came over to help with the house struck up a conversation. She said they had a good time and she told the wife that she likes me.

I just blurted out to my wife while we were all together that you (my wife) go, go and fly like an eagle. I still love you and go fly like an eagle, do what ever you think you need to do and I am sure that you will land to a place where it is where you are you. I and the kids will be ok and you just go ahead. Fly like an eagle.

We kissed as she left, it was a friendship kiss and to where I and she knew I was hers if she wanted. And that's where I left it at.

I then started my evening with the girl that was there after my wife left with all the kids. We had shots of tequila and lime and shrimp. The jumbo kind, with sauce. We danced to all the music and had a wonderful evening.

I got a letter in the mail from my lawyer. The court date is set.

Day 5

I just got home from work a little while ago. The wife watched the kids today. I usually don't work on the weekends.

As soon as I got here she was putting her things together and yawning and ready to go. She said she is not used to getting up so early in the morning. I said I have to get up at the crack of dawn every morning with the kids. Here she just had the kids overnight and during one day and she's wasted.

I got those emotional blues today. I am a lonely man. I asked her if she ever felt lonely. Why did I even ask her! Hell, I don't know. I am a lonely man even with three kids in the house.

I reminded my wife of our court date this month. I asked her what she wants out of the divorce again. To put it in a nutshell she wants to have a 3 bedroom house and wants me to provide her the income for it. In a round about way that is what she said.

I told her that I don't want any surprises from her at court. She said she hasn't talked to her lawyer in a while. I said well you better. I said I have been straight forward with you in all this and you better not be doing or setting up anything underhanded. She left. She will collapse in her room.

How in the heck do people do it? A divorce; it's like being branded. I mean, I don't care, it's nothing I am ashamed of. But now I am listed as maimed divorced parent. Or single parent.

I just got done with having the littlest boy sucking on a bar of soap. I heard him in the living room yelling and saying the F word and GD and son of a bitch and everything. That will not be tolerated in this house. Even from me, and how I could use it.

I have to say that the soap thing was an attention getter. I did not scream at him or anything. I calmly took him into the bathroom and he knew just what to do. Open wide. Insert bar. It isn't his way I think for what type of person he is.

He loves shrimp. I cooked up a big pot of it and he and I stood in the kitchen afterwards and ate the jumbo shrimp, all the while making conversation. I get through to him better in this type of setting than the yelling and strong arm tactics.

I talked with him about what kind of sauce we could concoct with what we had in the fridge. We made up some and experimented.

I am lonely. Deeply so. Damn it! I was so in a fix that I called my wife tonight just to talk. She said what do you need. I said, I'm lonely and I just wanted to talk. She laughed and said, "I only have a few minutes left on my cell phone time."

I closed with the tail between my legs kind of thing and said good night. She said she will call me tomorrow. I didn't say but tomorrow is too late. When one needs "that" one can't wait. A real friend wouldn't wait. So I have lost a lover and now a friend.

Life does come around again. What kind of life do I want? I want the one that I thought I had with my wife.

Oh. The torture, the pain, the pit of despair. To find out the real meaning and thoughts from actions of a love that one thought they shared.

I'll stop with the "oh woe is me," it doesn't help I know. But one does look for pity and a loving shoulder to lie upon and cuddle.

My knee is very good today. Actually, yesterday at work I didn't have to limp around anymore. I walked normally and with no pain. I am still keeping the appointment with the MR so as to fully make sure there isn't something simple to fix before it works into a lame knee.

Day 7

Even though my wife has stepped on us and caused
so much turmoil and terrible things in our lives I will wait.
Maybe 2 or 3 years. I will continue to travel through my
life and have a quality one with the kids. I will not be
overly mean and hateful to her. But the boundaries set
are ones that she will know.

Yes she may never come back to us. But to give life
a chance that's all I'm pursuing. Mainly for my kids and I.

Women. After the divorce that "she" wanted so much
I will engage in meeting other women and having dinner
and maybe dancing. I don't quite know how to put this to
the kids yet but it will be done with love.

My oldest has been given a pillow to punch when he
needs to get out his anger and the punching is only a few
days away. He expresses himself and his anger with
vulgar words and the mannerisms of one with frustrations.

Day 9

I have been thinking a lot about my predicament knowing that all of us have different ways of traveling our roads of life. I for one do not do the right things all the time.

I wrote a letter which my wife will read tomorrow while watching the boys. This is what I wrote:

My Dearest Wife,

But soon to be departed of that title. So sadly as it seems. * have wondered what would have been different if you and I had taken the plunge into what both of us really wants out of life and relationship marriage. Gone that way instead of the way it has gone.

My days are filled with responsibilities of getting the kids off to school and work and trying to make happiness for the little ones we brought into the world. Letting them grow up with fearless boyhood instead of grown up responsibilities that are now put upon them. It is just a different travel for them than what they were expecting. It is because of you and I that they have had a life altering change in their lives.

I do not write this to down you in any way. For you are at a crossroads in your life. I know that now. Please excuse me for taking so long in catching up with you.

Reflecting back upon our married life together. It has not been a bed of roses. Far from it. I have wanted only the best for you and I and the kids. But somehow failed in your eyes in that. Somewhere in your thinking emotional life that you did not confide in me, you gave up on me. Thought me a failure and not worth the time for working out. I understand this and ...well it works both ways in a relationship. I only wish you gave me a chance you didn't you know.

So you ran. Ran from the life you didn't understand for yourself. Feeling you can get all your answers elsewhere. All the while, the answers are found within. But you pursue your life for answers externally. Thinking that they come from other people. And the answers are right there within you.

Please, if this sounds like midlife crisis, just give it another word. For you are defiantly traveling a road. That road honey, takes time, space and disconnectedness. In our case from not only me but also your own children. Though not a normal divorce thing. It is something much more. And I know that. Because details of "why" has never been said. You don't know.

That is why I have decided to wait on you. For 2 to 3 years. Not succumbing to a new marriage or relationship that would jeopardize you and I. I love you more than that. I know you will not see this for your life and focus is not on us but you. I am now in a position to where I *will just carry on life with the kids and wait. That is the choice I made. I had plenty of offers to succumb to women... many women... but I know the value of you.*

So honey I wanted to take this time out in your life to tell you this. That I love you more than life itself.

The shit lawyers will take us through hell and back again. For that is their job. You and I will live with the law consequences. I want to live with supporting you through your journey, even if it is painful to me monetarily or time.

I was connected with you at one time and somehow that connectedness was severed by circumstances but rest assured that things change and people change and life improves by the changes we travel.

I love you dear. I want you more than life. I will wait for you and during that time of wait I will teach our children the value of the love from mother and father. I never ever put you down in front the kids. You can bank on that. Yes I have put up the shield of ...you having to earn your own way. And hard knocks in that respect ...you are feeling ...I'm sure.

I work, I play and although I do not do everything perfect I am still trying to provide the sustenance that our children and maybe someday you will be proud of.

You are my sunshine of my life. And even if the men you are with seem to give you the answers you like, look back to when I was your all, and what I have grown to become more than you ever wanted in a man that is yours. For keeps. Loving you and will wait,

This was the letter I posted in a sealed envelope taped to the fridge. It speaks of some but not all for that I am hoping will give her thinking thoughts along her way. I do not count on this letter making a big difference but will maybe influence her down the road. She knows of my wants and concerns but right now they are not in her. I hoped this letter would put her mind in a thinking phase.

This morning I read the letter and filed it away with my other writings. I did not leave it for her. She knows everything already so if she ever wants to come back, she already knows what I said in the past. I am not going backwards.

Drinking. Last night I had one margarita. That's it. I don't drink all the time, I don't have time.

I have been working weekends and overtime during the week. I get home late. Get the kids lovey dovey and look at their homework. Put them to bed. Mix a drink and go online for a while. Fall asleep around 12 and do it all over again.

I feel good and the knee is feeling much better.

Now my wife wants an old camera that I got a long time ago from her parents when they were going to throw it out. She was so adamant about wanting it in fear that the kids will get hold of it and break it up. I said why do you want it? She said because it was in my family. Huh?

I said OK and left it at that. She will be watching the kids today, tomorrow and all next week while they are on spring break.

Day 10

I'm glad its Friday. I can work on the clothes putting away this weekend. And the clean up in the yard. Our dog got into the garbage about a week ago and it's all over the yard.

The kids had fun with all the paint in the garage. I don't even want to go into there to see the mess they made.

This kinda sucks. It does suck!

For the last two days my wife has been watching the kids because they are off school for parents teachers conference. One would think that since she has three kids and knowing how my work schedule has been with working overtime and late hours that the house and clean up takes a nose dive, even further than it has already.

I would think she would clean up and help and all that. If not for me but for the kids. She hasn't done anything really. She did do some dishes and the upstairs bathroom but that's it.

She has a key to the other man's home and she said it's because she cleans his house.

So it comes down to me. Only me. If anything is going to happen it is because of me. Amen to that I guess. I still have a lot of stamina. I can go a long way I guess until I die.

I have found out how strong I really am in a lot of ways I didn't know. Emotionally strong. Physically strong. Kind. Not flying off the handle anymore for that doesn't accomplish anything.

Have I finally found out how to "Be"? Just Be? I didn't even know that. How unconscious of me. In some ways I wouldn't trade anything for what positive things are happening and will happen in my life. Yes I am lonely. Oh so lonely.

I miss the gentle touch of a woman's caress and me wrapping my hands around her face gently caressing and planting a gentle kiss in the dark. Those days I think will come. I have to speak truthfully. I have my own visualization of what all women are like.

Day 12

I've got a right to rant and rave lunacy too.

This day started with me having to go into work expecting just to finish up on a few details but that didn't work out too well. So it was back to the drawing board and now the heat was on. Whatever it takes we will do it.

The only problem was that my kids were at home with me calling them from time to time. I have my cell strapped to me all the time for them. It was getting dark so I took lunch, ran and got milk and cereal and ended up full shopping. Got home and we put the food away.

All the while I was wondering what I was going to do with the kids for the rest of the night. Who will watch them? My neighbor is a basket case these days. Can't count on her and she fell through on watching them.

The gal I have been seeing told my neighbor that I should get my wife because it is her kids! So it was with great distain that I called my wife. Several times too.

Left messages on her cell phone. I was going to give it up and just stay home when she called.

She said what do you want. Did you call? I said yes. I explained to her that I will have to pull an all-nighter at work and tomorrow too. I have no one to watch the kids. She said well it's going to be an hour or so. I (like a dummy) asked what are you doing there. She said, huffily, I have been busy and need time out. I was hoping to have this weekend by myself.

I thought to myself in the split second before I spoke again, she is by herself, no responsibilities. Free time to go where ever she wants and does. Goes to downtown clubs. Has a social life and can come and go as she pleases. Sleep till noon. All that.

I cannot do that. Have not done that in ... I can't remember. Huh! And she's giving me the business about watching the kids.

I took my oldest with me to work. He wanted to see what I did. We hung out and that was neat. Called it quits at 11pm and will pick it up at 9am tomorrow. I figure I will be done before dark and be home. I will stay in contact with the kids by phone.

The kicker here was when I got home before I called my wife, my neighbor's little girl was here and fell on the patio and got a gash on her hand that I really think needed 2 maybe 3 stitches.

I had to go and find her mom who was home lollygagging on the phone when she was going to watch the kids. Her mom decided that she will stitch it up herself. That's nuts.

I offered to take her and pay for the emergency room visit and all. The mom was too tired to take the time to do that.

With all that said, I don't need any of that from people. None! I feel caught and caged. Things will only get done if I get them done. Women! who needs them! So far all I've gotten are headaches and heartaches from them.

I will wait for my wife. Why? Why wait for someone who now screws you in a different way? I don't know what I'm going to do. That's still to be determined.

All I know is that I don't want this to go on and on. With me picking up the pieces from other people's lives. Their garbage and trash I have to clean up. I think I'll put it all on the curb.

My wife is definitely off the deep end. I think the reason she helped me last night and today was out of guilt. She knows she is trashing many lives for her own selfish wants. No matter how it kills the kids' spirit and this will have life long effects on them. All because she wants to go out and live her own life like we are not existing. How can someone get so far in their heads to rationalize what they are doing is OK?

It is catching up with me. The responsibility. Burning candles at both ends. Trying to be mommy and daddy. I think I am doing a pretty good job so far. At least I know my limits and that will be that I need help.

I would love to leave her out of it. I have to do some planning, summer is coming on. We will be divorced and she will probably no longer help me cause her idea of divorce is likened to never having known the former spouse. I don't exist and so she doesn't have to do anything anymore.

I don't know how to explain it fully. She is with this guy and has his house key and cleans his house. She says she likes to help people. But when it comes to me there is none. What did I ever do? Nothing. Nothing at all. That is the crazy part of all this.

I ran out of my antidepressants yesterday. I have been taking them for 8 months now. I have the shakes.

Will have to go to the Dr's tomorrow and have her write a scrip. I don't want to get off of them until after the divorce. I'm kind of afraid.

Day 13

Well it's 6pm and I went and got my Rx at 1pm today. I took two 150mg and went home for the rest of the day. The kids and wife were not home which was good. I felt woozy and wobbly until they kicked back in. I was out for two hours.

The wife arrived with the kids and left immediately. Said twice to me good-by so I would have to respond.

She went out and bought new shoes for the boys and rented a video game for them. The kids mentioned that she is getting a 3 bedroom apartment this week maybe. All this on a minimum wage 40 hour work week.

Her lawyer did say to her that if she didn't have a place big enough for the kids and her when we went to court that it would look bad on her.

My question is that she didn't mention anything to me that she was getting an apartment this week. I fear the worst will come out of her and her lawyer when we go to court. I have been straight with her all along and have told her that.

If she does this fucking bull in court and tries to screw me I will forever never forgive her. I don't think I could. It would take a lot of whatever to get over that mountain and it will be hers to hurtle.

I am home with the heebee jeebies and no one to talk to. So I will write my thoughts instead.

I just feel so lonely. But can't and will not let that bring me down. I have to keep going and hold my guns. I did not have time today to look for a nanny but will tomorrow.

I don't like to talk with my neighbors anymore. I am contemplating after this is all over and settled down I may want to move. I will stay in state because of work but I don't like this place anymore.

My wife went to the doctor today in preparation to get her tubes tied. She said to me the other day you don't like that do you!! I fired back and said the only reason you want to do that is so you won't have to worry any more about getting pregnant and so you can go out and mess around with men.

She said that right in front of my kids. She said she was doing this so she won't have anymore of you's as she was pointing to my youngest son.

If I keep this anger up I think I will make it through to the end of the divorce because I did not want this divorce. I would much prefer that she go out and do all the crazy things she wants to do and get it over with and hit rock bottom somewhere and contact me then. Only then can we start.

Day 17

Yesterday the kids were all gone and the aloneness was too great but today was another day. Stayed home from work and the kids and I installed a new water softener in the well house. My water is now a lot softer.

I can't believe I drank half a fifth of tequila. But I did. I rarely do that. Is it becoming a problem? No. I don't drink every day. I am just lonely.

I went for a walk today which was nice. The weather is turning nice. It will be in the 70's for the weekend. Time to clean the yard.

This evening the boys and I are going out to eat somewhere. They will choose.

Why don't I just come out and say it. I hate my life. I hate what's been going on that never seems to stop. I hate that I cannot seem to get my act together with my life so as to enjoy it. Get to a point that pain will be gone.

I seem to be living life in the raw. No clothes. No nothing for protection. Come... Take me... as I charge through this life. But now it's all in the mind. Emotions, feelings, the fire within. I burn for life. My life! Why don't I just go out and grab it?

Could it be the stagnation of waiting for someone who is not worth it? We all come to a point individually, where we GET IT. Well I GOT IT.

I need ME right now and that's all. I know that now. I feel it and it gnaws on me all the time. Forget about everything and do what your gut and your heart have been telling you all along but have been bucking it.

I know what I need to do and the time has arrived. I cannot deny what is truth as I see it in my mind and heart.

So. It is here. Staring back at me. Myself!

So I take it now. For now has arrived.

Day 20

Sometimes one drives themselves to extremes. That's ok for me it seems. I, in the end, am (as I look back) much more refined and focused in my life. Especially when I am not alone. I have 3 little boys too.

It took me only a second as I watched in silence, at my two youngest boys sleeping on the sofa. Them laying there sitting up sleeping with one's mouth open and another's heavy nasal breathing.

In those seconds, I realized that they have no one but me. Those little human beings. The feeling from that sight and thought gave me such a direction, a meaning in my life. A feeling of okayness. A good feeling it was.

I have to get off my dead ass and become more to my kids.

It was a warm day. The kids two times got wet, head to toe in the pond and all blamed each other of who pushed who.

I really only scolded them because of their new shoes that mom bought them only a week ago.

They all got baths and they did the dishes and cleaned up the living room. I just said it had to be done. When I got back from the store it was done, mostly. It was nice my oldest and I standing side by side finishing the dishes. Talking.

So I guess its coming along slowly but headed in a good direction. Tomorrow will be clothes put away day.

I did get that knot in my stomach earlier today like when this all started. But it did not last. It was like a reminder of what I don't want.

I feel much better today. I was so pushed down because of my procrastination. I had an interrogatory that was supposed to be completed weeks ago, but I didn't do anything about it. Why? I don't know.

I finally took the step and got hold of my lawyer today and took all my financial papers down to his office and we went over the interrogatory step by step. Half hour it was done.

He called my wife's lawyer and he said no problem if it was late and that the court trial date is set. My wife and I do not have to show up in court tomorrow. I am so relieved. I now have another chance and I need to please don't blow it!

My lawyer says that she will not get anything from the divorce as far as alimony. All she will probably get is half of the 401K plan at my work. She will end up paying child support.

I just can't wait till it's over. Done with. What she is doing has become an irritation to me now. That's funny to feel like that.

I am taking the kids to the park to play basketball.

Day 24

Today is my birthday. I am 51 years young. The only ones who said happy birthday were two people at work.

My day was spent working half a day and making copies of financial paperwork and delivering them to my lawyer's office. We sat together and chatted about laws in the state concerning divorce. My lawyer said that when he talked to my wife a while back that she seemed like someone that wakes up each morning with a different head. I said yes she does not know what she is doing day to day. She lives day to day.

I will most likely pay alimony but for only 2 years. Two years are long enough for someone to get their pay scale up. He said that she will have to pay some child support and that it still looks like I will get sole custody.

She has been visiting the schools and taking my sons out of class to talk with them for 10 minutes and then sending them back to class.

I told my lawyer this and I concur that this is disruptive to a child. All in all I don't want to wait for the trial. My lawyer said that after her lawyer sees that I am not a gold mine an offer from them will be forthcoming. So we might just settle out before trial. I will not budge. She will have to cave.

It's my birthday and I wonder if there was a serious problem happening in my family the year I was born? This is so much like a French surrealistic film. Like an acid trip at times. Unreal.

But I am not like that anymore. I hurt, yes, but there is a large portion of me that is an adult now. Did I say that? I will tag along with reality and make my dreams become that!!

WOW !!! what a birthday with all the glitz. I am frying chicken and having mashed potatoes and corn. I think we will all like that.

As far as the booze goes... too late I had one mixed drink. The radio is playing country music. Vince Gill... oh how he brings the most out of one.

I talked to the wife tonight on the phone and she is going to take the kids with her overnight in her one room apartment. I told her that I will be gone overnight working on an engine rebuild with a friend of mine. She can use the house and I will not be back.

She made the big stink about me meeting her at a gas station to make the transfer of the kids. I said no! You will come and get them from home. She ranted and raved about how she will contact her lawyer and make me do that. I quietly and lovingly talked to her about the law. It has to do with safety and all that. That is why one will pick up the children and drop them off at the domicile. She seemed to understand and I left it at that.

Strange things we want to do on our birthdays, huh? Work on an engine. She said also that the reason she does not want to come to the house is because it is her house too. It hurts her to come to it. Knowing ... what?

Something she will have to come to grips with. It seems she so wants the house without me and just with the kids and live her life the way she sees it right now. I am sorry. She cannot kick me out of her life so easily. I have a feeling I am staring at her in her mind all the time. I wonder what feelings that entrap her cycle in?

I just don't know.

Day 27

It's been a good weekend. I went out Saturday around noon and stayed overnight in the city. I was originally going to stay at a friend's house but that fell through so I ended up at a couple of clubs. Good rock and roll music. Had a good time meeting people.

I came home Sunday around 1 pm. My wife started to leave immediately but I caught her at her car and said I have to talk to you about two things.

I first asked her was it a good idea that you have been coming to the kids' school and taking them out of class and talking to them for 5 or 10 minutes and then sending them back to class? Don't you think this is interrupting their day? How do you think they feel after, and having to go back to class for the rest of the day? She said it is just for a few minutes and she didn't see how it was bad.

The other thing I told her is that my oldest told me that the guy she's with had a talk with him and said that he went through a divorce and feels really bad and that his mom is helping him and he needs her and all that.

I told my wife how do you think that is affecting our son? Don't you think that is bad? I do not want any influence on any of our children with any of that. They are our kids and don't need that. This is your problem and keep it that way.

She insisted that there was no way that he could have talked to our son like that. I said it happened while he was over there and beside the point. It's my son's perspective on this and that's the important thing.

She was angry and I left it at that. She drove away.

I know that I am a person that can and could have provided my wife with all the love, support, a good happy life and she knew that. But she decided that she didn't want to put forth the effort on her part. For she knows that I would. She is the loser in all this. I know who I am. I feel good about myself that's how far I've come.

I and my children are the important ones and that is where it will stay. She kisses this guy in front of the kids and all. This is just eventually going to damage her relationship with her kids in the long run.

She just keeps on digging her hole deeper and deeper. I doubt now that she will ever come out. She will stay the way she is and her pride and lack of dealing with her inner self will keep her in one place for the rest of her life. That's the way I see it.

Day 30

It's been an interesting day to say the least. The past couple of days my lower back was giving me hell. It got worse and worse. This morning I woke up and screamed with every movement I gave to my body. My legs were numb all the way down to the balls of my feet. The kids missed the school bus. So here I was barely making it to the bathroom.

It was time for me to go to the emergency room. I was getting ready to do that when my oldest son hands me the phone. He called mommy. I didn't need this I thought. I don't want her help.

But I answered the phone. She said what's wrong? I said my back is out and so painful and I am going to the emergency room. She said I am nearby and will be there soon.

She came. Got me into her car and took me to the hospital. It was a long wait once we got there! While waiting she can see me in so much pain. She said do you want me to rub it. She did but wouldn't touch my skin. It felt good and she did it several times while waiting.

I got looked at and was given a diagnosis of sciatic nerve problems. They wrote me 3 scripts. She left before I was done to pick up the kids. Came back when I was done.

While driving home the kids were acting up and she tells them that now it is two spankings when we get home. If you want more then just keep it up. We got home and she spanked them except for the youngest. They were love taps really. Then she started to bark out orders for the kids to get going on clean up. They did the dishes and cleaned up the living room. After which they could still not turn on the electronics, games and such.

I meanwhile was getting dinner on. During this her cell phone rings and the kids dive for it. She screams out, don't touch it. Let it ring. A few minutes later she says she has to go.

She kisses all the kids goodbye but our oldest keeps insisting on going with her for an overnight. She gives him no answer. She goes outside. Me thinking she is gone by now. But no. She comes in with her cell phone strapped to her jeans now instead of her purse. Goes over to the cupboard and gets dishes out and starts setting the table.

We sit and our youngest says the blessing. We eat and clear the table. She has one cigarette then says she has to go now. Meanwhile our oldest is hounding her to stay over night with her. She finally says no. She gets into her car and goes.

So now. What do I make of all this? Actions? She did come in my hour of need. Took care of whatever needed to be. But in the end she chose to go to the other man's house. She did take off work to help me.

I had to hold back today from opening my heart to her. I did say three times, thank you. What about role reversal here. It was so prevalent to me. Me, the nurturer and now she the disciplinarian. But in the end she chose to deep six and leave for the other man.

The pills I got are helping me a lot now. I just can't lay down. That's how I am going to sleep I guess. Sitting up?

I will be off of work till Monday. I hope my problem goes away by then. Back problems that is.

I bought pads (Kotex) for her before we got home. I asked her don't you have any money at all? She smiled and shook her head. I buy her pads and hell, while I'm at the store for milk anyways I pick her up a 12 pack of diet cola. And while she's not looking I stuff a 20 dollar bill in her purse.

I know. I still love her. Big deal. My life will not be the worse for doing that. I kept my heart guarded throughout the day. For even though she did those nice things helping me out in the end she would go back to what she wants. And that is not to see me or come to this house because when she calls she only talks to the boys and doesn't talk to me. She probably doesn't have anything to say.

She is starting to call each night now around 9:00 to say goodnight to them. I of course am not included with that. Interesting how much anger she has and she so much takes it out on me. But it doesn't bother me anymore. I know it's her problem not mine.

It will be interesting when it comes down to maybe one week before the divorce trial. She already knows that I didn't want the divorce but she wanted it. Can, will she go all the way? Probably. Because a long time ago it seems when this first happened she said she wants/needs that kind of disconnect from me to see if she wants me.

Day 35

I have been off work now since Friday. It is painful to just get up and walk from the bed to the kitchen or anywhere for that matter. The doctors must have a problem of giving one high dosages of narcotic medicines. I ended up again doubling the dosage that was recommended just to get some relief.

I will have to call my doctor and have her write another Rx because I am going to be out tomorrow. I have an MRI scheduled on Wednesday morning.

I still get up and get the kids off to school. My oldest has said that he will stay home and help me. I am thinking of having him stay home tomorrow. He takes a lot of weight on his shoulders since this all happened not only with my ailments but what the wife has done. He so much wants and feels that what he does will make things right in our family. Plus at the same time he is going through puberty. This might be a time to make this into a good learning experience for him and I both.

My wife knows what I'm going through. She hasn't said or done anything at all. She doesn't care. Nor has she called. Which is ok. She has made it clear that I and the kids are on our own by her actions. So again, I must think of her as dead. To move on with my life as if one has lost their loved one through death.

I couldn't even drive to get some milk and bread today. Tomorrow, I will, I guess, have my son go into the store and purchase milk and bread on his own. I know this is another chance where he and I can really bond. I take those advantages when they come.

There is more to this all than meets the eyes and mind I think. Through all this I continue to want to do the right things. Guidance from God and friends give me strength for another day. For life moves on without us if we let it.

I wonder sometimes if my wife reads my journal. It doesn't matter I guess. For her actions speak for themselves. Her actions are one of selfishness and of denial. That is where she is stuck. Maybe forever.

Day 37

I went and got MRI and X-rays yesterday. I came home and right away got a phone call from Dr. Said he wants me to go right away to a neurosurgeon in the city and can I go now.

I went with oldest son and the Dr. gave me an examination. Showed me the MRI's with protruding disk and bone fragment pinching my nerve. He said you need surgery so he set it up for today at 12 noon. He is concerned about the bone fragment that might sever the nerve.

It is 2 hrs away until surgery. I have no one to watch the kids. So...my wife will be watching them. Also her car battery is bad and it needs to be replaced. She insisted that she will get a new battery in two weeks.

She said she doesn't want anything from me and bla bla bla. Guilt trip towards me. Well it ain't working. This morning I got the kids off to school and oldest wants to stay with me again through all this. We stopped over at wife's apartment. Woke her up and I watched her through the doorway as she put on her make up and such. Her long beautiful legs.

Oh how I wanted to just grab her in my arms and look into her eyes and say honey lets stop all this stuff. Get rid of that pride that keeps you from talking and working on our relationship.

That didn't happen. That was all in my mind. I had to come to reality.

We drove both cars to my house and she is taking me to the hospital. She called someone and I know who it is.

I know this is going to be ok. I will get the surgery and mending will take about two weeks. Will write more when I get out of the hospital.

Day 38

Just got home from hospital. It went well. I now can stand up straight with no pain. The surgeon did it arthroscopically. I stayed overnight and got out by 1pm today. I have to take physical therapy for a week or so because lower legs don't seem to want to cooperate. The kids are at school now so the house is empty.

I do have some things I want to write about. My wife took me to the hospital with my oldest. While waiting in the foyer for a bed, my wife mentioned that she had to change her appointment for her tubes getting tied. I said I will take you when you go. She said no, her boyfriend is going.

Now. I'm on the edge here! I am taking care of these kids. Raising them. She's out ...doing!!!

I didn't need that! I got up walked to another chair and hid my tears. Then I got up and tried to walk out and have a cig. I heard as tripped and fell to the floor, Oh don't get so mad. I got up and somehow made it outside.

My son came out and said they are ready for you. I hobbled in and undressed in the prep room. My wife looks at me and says you want me to leave? I didn't say anything I think.

The anesthesiologist comes in and goes through the what he is going to do. I make a joke that this time I want to know when I'm going under. Meanwhile he is putting two shots into my IV. They come and wheel me into the operating room. There are a lot of people.

Now really buzzed and fighting the drug and going under fast I hear myself yelling and telling all that would hear about the story about my wife and what she did and the children. All of it. The last thing I remember is him looking down at me putting another shot in my IV.

I awoke in my room about 4pm I guess. Last night the kids showed up and gave me hugs and kisses. The kind that gushes tears from one's eyes.

My wife did nothing as I should expect. She just sat there.

Today I am antsy to get out but slow it is with waiting for all the paperwork. My wife comes and waits with me, silently. And silent the long drive home too. She got into her car and left. I did say thanks to her though.

My house is as I left it. Messy. I vow to pay someone to come once or twice c week now to clean. I do not want to depend upon her ever again. So I will do my homework and have things set up with someone else in case things like this come about. She has really shown her true colors.

The world does look different today. It looks and feels like independence day!

Day 39

I slept on it and still feel the same. Knowing for sure that it is all over between my wife and I. No one treats or does what she did when one is in such a state going into surgery and all.

I am not mad or anything at her anymore. That is gone. I only have a feeling of knowing that she is nothing to me anymore and not worth any thought from me about her and her problems of any kind.

I feel relieved actually. I feel good and at rest like a big sack of woe is off my shoulders. With this, I have now the opportunity to really live my life happily with me and the kids like it should be. It's like I never had her in the first place. That kind of feeling. I don't even have to be her friend anymore. Because she's not. She is like someone that one meets that one doesn't want to meet again. That sort of realization and feeling.

I know I will see her from time to time because of the kids. But she will be a stranger that I don't care to know anything about.

It's a feeling that I feel good about. Today is really the first day of my life. I am free.

Today was spent going out with kids and getting them new jeans and summer shirts and all. They really needed them. They look so bummy all the time to me. We stayed gone all day.

We got back and had some leftover pizza and I fell asleep watching TV.

We are going to church tomorrow. It is something I have wanted to do for some time but didn't.

I still can't believe how my perspective and outlook has changed since the other day. It's like I woke up or something. Looking at life anew. It's a feeling I can't seem to put words to. I like it and it feels good. I am now looking forward to the next day. Not as drudgery, but with possibilities and excitement.

Day 45

As I write this opening I hear the crunching of the gravel under the weight of my wife's car with all the kids in it driving out through the driveway. The crunching weight of everything that I seem to only feel and not her.

Now I am alone. Just the whirr of the computer's blower do I hear. The click and clack of the keys as I pound out the words of my life that only I will see. It ain't effin fair. Well there is nothing written that says life is fair.

My wife is taking the kids out tonight for pizza and to watch Scooby Do on the tube. She came in here with her head hanging low and forcing herself to say. "I came to ask for money so I can take the kids out for pizza." I didn't answer right away. I just moved around the house. Walking.

I was in my bedroom and I called out honey! Come in here. She sat on my bed with the clothes all mussed around. I asked what are your plans for this weekend? She said, when, tonight?

I played her game and said yes and for Easter. She said I don't have a big enough place for the kids to stay I will probably stay at my apartment on Easter.

I said I want you to know that you are invited for dinner. She said no. I grinned and said I wanted to at least invite you. But if you want to stay at your place and feel woe is me go ahead. That's your problem.

We ended up in the kitchen at the table like most conversations end up at. I wrote her a $40 check. Put it into her purse along with a music tape I made. I said since music seems to reach you, maybe this will.

She asked me if I had a beer. I got up and was getting her one and she said I can get it! I opened up both bottles and handed hers and said cheers. We sat there small talking (I was leading her on to see where her mind was at), for some time. Smoking cigs for at least 45 minutes. I then said you better get going if you're going to take the kids out tonight. She said she would have them back around noon tomorrow.

I kissed each one and they gave me hugs. I said to my wife, have a good night. She said, you too.

Now all through this contact with the wife I was happy, assertive, and at ease. I smiled and laughed and was not mechanical. She on the other hand, when she asked for money was bent over and down looking like a dog with its tail between its legs. After she was more talkative and up beat.

She never ever said thanks for the money. She completely forgot. She was so thinking about other things. Like getting out of there. Amazing how she feels so terrified to be around me. For no reason now.

I have been the good husband. Not the best. But never ever any verbal or physical abuse. Always uplifting her to a pedestal of woman and wife and mother.

I'm going to have a few beers and continue on the clean up of the house and listen to music at max volume. I wish I had a friend to come over and join me. In the beers that is.

I think I'm doing pretty good considering where I was. I still listen to that little voice that tells me what's right and what's wrong. For it's the choices that I make too.

Day 46

I did tie one on last night.

I do know that my wife has no idea why she doesn't want to come to our home or see me. It's just the pain she feels I think. I can speculate a lot. But it would do no good. She can't stand not having money so she can have a big enough place for the 3 kids and her to go to and not any money to buy them things. She said if I had a big enough place right now the kids would be spending Easter with me!

That's when I asked her why do you hate me so much? She had no answer. Just silence. Then she came out with if I had a big enough place the kids would be with me for Easter.

She is waiting and hoping that when we go to court that she will get alimony and all kinds of money from me. She also hates it that I have control over the kids with the temporary order. She is so mad and feels that I took her motherly controls away from her. She told me that in front of the kids too. All I know is that she has a long road to hoe. By herself. After the divorce and she gets nothing what is she going to be left with? It will be final then and she will have to deal with it.

I have to reiterate that this isn't about her anymore. It's about me now. Me and the kids getting on with our lives.

I am so happy that I still have that unending barrel of love in tact. Instead of indiscriminately spreading it around like I did before. I give a little thought to how and where I use it now.

I still use my gifts and grow with them. For I like the nature of the man I see emerging from all this. I still have my personal bumps along that road but it doesn't keep me from my aim in the crosshairs of direction.

I just got back from picking up the kids from their mom's place. I was out getting the Easter basket things. This year I went with the ready made. But they have big remote control cars and slot cars and basketballs in them. I got other things to enhance the baskets. Like the white chicken that poops out candy when you push its legs down. Cool.

I found a good leg of lamb and will cook that for dinner tomorrow. The boys and I will be attending church.

I picked up the boys and as I was walking towards my car, I asked the wife. Hey, I'm asking you for a date tonight. It will be setting up the Easter baskets and filling the plastic eggs for the hunt on Easter. That's if you want to have a date with this old man here, smiling. She didn't say anything but nodded.

After her kissing each child in the car and while I was walking around to get in I said are you going to church? She said probably not. I said we are having leg of lamb, (of which I outlined the menu), and you are invited. The kids want you to come too. She didn't say anything.

While driving home I asked the kids if they asked mom to come to dinner and middle son says yes but she said no. He said that mommy told him she will probably go over to boyfriend's house for Easter. I asked him how he felt about that. He said it sucks and doesn't like it. That's where I left it.

So it is her choice again. It is set up. She knows. Hears those voices that tell her what is right and what is wrong. And she will make a choice. These and many more will and have defined her life, her relationship with humanity and most important, with herself. I wish and pray that she starts making good choices.

No one needs to tell me her choices are ok and that it is her life and all. I will just note them and make some of my choices that will protect the kids.

Sleep is far from me this night before Easter morning. Cigarettes, beer, and tequila has been soaked up. My mind is ajar with thoughts of God, wife, children, and what is left of me.

The "ME" is what I have been wrestling with this evening. The effect of what my wife has done has positioned my mind in a state of questioning. Questioning myself and second-guessing as to why she has pursued the path she has taken. Always at the forefront is the possibility of something that I have done to cause her choices that take her away from me? I can find some but not enough to cause this great change in her. Ones that negate everything that we had ever talked about in our lives.

I look and see the forest. I then look and see the trees. I even look at the leaves. The texture of the bark on the trees. Have I missed something? Is my touch of skin not tender enough? Was my gentle deep looking into her eyes and softly cooing the affirmation of love and respect not good enough? Was my climbing the ladder of success and monetary increases not good enough?

I gave of myself unselfishly my whole of what was me. In many different ways. Ways that were balanced. For I know that the sum is the parts of many. Change is ongoing. Like a river that never stands still. We also have those tributaries that are like still waters of rest. Which is the balance one needs for wholeness.

This isle of rest maybe my wife never had. This again is second-guessing. To reach her to "help her" is a many varied endeavor. She is likened to a chimpanzee that has its hand in a jar but can't figure out how to release its hand to get its hand out.

The mirrors I look at which are me reflect a person that was complex but simple. The fire of life and its pressures have forged those mirrors into facets of diamonds.

The reflections are much purer than before. Like starting with the unknown, I have ended up with the known. Like learning the letter "A", and traveling to "Z."

Am I complete? No. Far from it. But am sure of my "ME" that I was unsure of at the beginning. So I look at this person that I married and bonded I thought with as one that doesn't understand the deepness to the degree of my love for her. Or she does but doesn't want that kind of love. Again second-guessing.

I do know that nothing is perfect and I am far from it. But the energy of wanting to is shown by the continuance of trying. And having fun at it at the same time. For to work and not have fun most of the time is not work. Really.

The light with the heavy. The balance. The Ying and the Yang. God and the Devil. It is personal. But true.

Day 47

It's 6:30 and the boys are up having candy for breakfast. I am having a good strong cup of coffee.

The sun is up and it looks clear and going to be a beautiful day. I did something a little different this year. I got the ready made baskets that have as the main thing in it is a large toy. Like a slot car racing set. Remote control cars. Sports things and army toys and such.

My wife didn't show up last night for the date. I didn't think she would. Oh well her loss. And she's not here to experience the wonderment and happiness of the kids as they each came to me and said, Happy Easter and He is risen. They remembered that!!!

I must be doing something right. We are going to church this morning. After that is the cooking of the leg of lamb. That's my fun. I love to cook. The kids are up to leg of lamb. It was surprising. At least that's what they said.

I am keeping away from downer thoughts today. At least I'll try. I am going to call my niece and sisters and have the kids talk to grandparents.

Our dog will get the leg of lamb bone. I got all the kids new flowered shirts to wear for church.

My oldest sons know that there is no Easter bunny. The oldest gave me the high five on that one.

Day 48

I was bumbling around at times this Easter with anger at my wife for not ever coming to see/experience/enjoy the kids in the Easter morning family time. Nor even coming for the Easter dinner that is a family tradition. Going to church too. Not even a phone call.

Her car was gone from her apartment. The kids saw and even said where she was. I could see and feel their disappointment.

I guess the important thing is that I expected this from her but was hoping all the same. That's the difference from how I handle things now than before.

Everyone tells me and explains to me that it is all over between her and I and she will never be back. I guess I know that but am not fully there in my mind yet. It will come but don't know how yet.

I am more concerned about the kids and how they will take the finality of that. It's just that the two younger

75

ones might turn out thinking that this is an ok thing that it's natural. Because that's all they know. True, after they grow up they will know the difference. But still, all I can do is lead by example.

I think I know where my wife's anger is coming from. She expected me to cave in, to give up, when she moved out and refused to help. I didn't cave in.

I didn't go nuts like she thought I would. I am keeping everything going. It was hard at the beginning. Oh crap. Was it hard. It still is but I'm getting better all the time.

The only hurtle that I really have now is a cosmetic one. That is with cleaning up and keeping the house in order.

The rest of it I think the most important things are going well. That is time with the kids. Homework. Reading, Play and such. Summer is coming on and outside activities will be more.

I don't think I will be seeing my wife much anymore. That is her way of getting back at me, she thinks. In retrospect, I am better when she is not around. This coming around once in a while actually upsets my life, kids included, though they need to see their mom.

She said that if she had money and a bigger place that the kids would be at her place for Easter and not here at home.

I know that her lawyer sent my lawyer an offer. I expect to hear about it this coming week. It's probably asking for the moon. She knows that she will be hit up for paying a lot of money for the kids' child support. She wants all but 1K of the tax refund this year which is approx. 4K.

She tells me and expects me to jump. Well so much for her lack of assertiveness problem that she said she had a while back. Along with saying I just need to move out for a little while so I can figure things out. Sitting all the kids down and telling them that and saying she would be back in about 4 months.

The only truth that she has said so far is she wants a divorce. She even told me that she didn't want anything but visitation rights. Along with the other men in her life since her moving out and her insistence of involving them with our children sealed her fate.

After the divorce it will be different. I will have no control over who she introduces to our children I know. I do know that she is so tired of having to keep low-key and cleaning up her act like her lawyer told her to do.

The one thing she will not do is give up seeing and living with her new man and taking my two oldest ones over there sometimes. That's going to bite her in the butt in court if it comes to that. Her lawyer probably doesn't know that she is doing that. But the kids do and my lawyer does.

Sometimes I'm still like a little boy in the way I deal with all this. I tend to forgive and forget easily. And want to play the next day. I'm not doing this of course. I have to check that at my mind's door. Just realize that I have that in me. And it's actually a good thing I think. In this case, I won't use it.

Well it's after 4am and the clock will be ringing at 5:30 to get up. I did it again. Oh well. I have an extra long candle to burn at both ends. It's good that we are starting back at church again. I see it already in the kids and their behavior. It has made a positive impact there. They like it. What can I say?

My back is healing well. I have no pain at all. My feet went from numb to now feeling tingling. I can now bend my toes up and am getting better mobility and strength in them. I still walk somewhat like a penguin. I don't use the walker anymore. What a bump in the road the back thing was.

My oldest hugged the toilet most of the night. 24 hr stomach crud. The only ones that will get it next is the littlest guy and me. Oh boy. Can't wait.

The leg of lamb dinner was great.

I feel one of those life emotional changing weeks coming on. I have Travis Tritt songs playing: "Here's A Quarter (Call Someone Who Cares)," "Anymore," "Tell Me I Was Dreaming," and "Can I Trust You With My Heart?" And least but not last, "The Whiskey Ain't Working."

The sun is out but it's cloudy in my mind. I found myself looking on the web at e-harmony.com. It was actually interesting reading about what other women are looking for. Most of what I read came down to One Woman, One Man.

They aren't looking for a ready-made family though. Especially one with three young boys. Oh well. Dates will be fun I guess. When that ever happens. I am not ready for that now anyways. I'm just lonely. To cuddle on the sofa watching a Fred Astaire or one of those laughable Danny Kay movies.

To talk softly to someone so close that you can feel the heat from their face. Smell the make-up or even the scent of what kind of face soap they used. A sweet soft conversation even about that. I know this is what women all want to hear huh? "The One And Only You" can make that change in me. You are the one and only you...

My oldest son is going to take a short course in HTML and web design. Also graphics design. The school sent some paperwork home and I am signing him up for it. Maybe he can teach me something.

Oh no. "Tell Me I Was Dreaming" just came on. Crap! Let me find that worm at the bottom of that bottle. No! It's the middle of the day. Can't do that. All this is like an acid trip.

I once was stuck (I thought), on a white bright sandy beach all day. I thought (I had myself convinced), that I knew how many grains of sand there were on the beach. The sun and its rays were a rainbow that I could walk on. The sensitivity of water in my pores of my skin as I walked into the water. Opening my eyes under the salty water. Seeing the molecules of life in the water. Life was alive.

That was a long time ago and life is alive just like that, now, without any effects from drugs. If one looks. Half with a mind of a child. Youth. I don't think I'll ever get rid of that. This molecule that is I in this sea of humanity has many new things to see and experience. Because the universe is very big. Why limit myself to a narrow spec of it.

There I go again. What in the hell am I saying?

I just glanced over the room and there on the nightstand is the Easter basket we made for mom. She didn't even have the decency to come over! Just as well.

I just took the CD of Martina McBride out of the basket along with a box of gourmet chocolates. It's the CD with Concrete Angel on it.

I'm tired of living in this box. Oh no! There I go again. Up and down. In and out. Forward and backwards. What in the hell did I miss? Nothing!!!! I traded institutionalized depth of learning for life's learning. The mixture of both I think. I have to be truthful here. For I have had both. There isn't anything like taking a sabbatical. "My heart's not ready for the rocking chair."

Am I off my rocker? No. I feel one of those life's emotional changing weeks coming on. Let's move to a close here. I am ok. Life with me and the massaging and integrating of my emotional and critical thoughts will end me in a place where I will have my heart in tact and my youth and myself as I am functioning socially. For I do not want to be so far out that no one understands me. I want to be left with life worth associating with molecules in this humanical universe. A new word, "humanical."

Knowledge brings peoples together but we should always remember individuals are essential. And must be coped with. Not coped with by anything goes. But now I enter a different realm, which is spiritual. I am not ready for that. For I am biased. Not really.

I've been around and feel I integrated enough with the common humanity to get enough feeling that right is right and wrong is wrong. And it comes from the same higher being.

I feel I am in one of those life emotional changing weeks that are coming on.

I think that Easter basket was for me. But I don't think I can wear that blouse with the orchid on the front of it though. The Easter card will be thrown into my drawer of memories. I wish I could write better.

I will stock up on my life's experiences. Aggravated bumps along the way that can't be crossed or seemingly enough power to jump the moguls. I seemingly can't ignore them but meet them and work through them. To ignore them would have them decrease the quality of life my life, and they would only show up again but much more intense. Sounds like a midlife crisis.

There are some things that one should not pass up. Push to the side. Submerge into their gray matter. To do so would be entering into expanding the pain which comes upon one to others that love you. There is a point of self destructiveness that kills all of the love that's been built and what we're all searching for in the first place.

Now I am on Vince Gill music. It's so nice having a computer that can multitask. Playing music in stereo at the same time. With equalizers and all that.

Remember the promise you wear on your left hand cheating no companion for a real ladies man. Remember the sweet wine and the softness of her lips when you said I really do. That eye to shaky knee eye love that you made. Think, feel, relive. Now the slightness I made of shaky knees.

If it was that then what did that mean? Maybe a longer courtship? A more of knowing yourself? To take a gamble on maybe thinking that all the pieces will come together and work themselves out over time. Wow!

And then there are little lives involved later on. That, "that is coming from my situation sort of." I knew what I wanted but didn't give our relationship enough piercing of challenging engagement that washed out many incompatibilities that would maybe be shown our individual hearts that we grieve at not being right for each other.

Ok. I'm rolling off my rocker again. I just ran out of words. My kid's just bungled in from school with hugs and reports of their most important life's trials. Come on let's show them how important their own life's struggles are.

I am caught between the cross fire of unknown enemies which are part of me that I don't know yet.

Day 50

Can't sleep tonight. It's 3 am and I am so tired. I have been wrestling with my inner self about something for the last three days. I just wonder what I am putting to rest this time, for many things are tied to letting go.

I think it has something to do with my heart and mind having a war without me. I have a feeling I don't care anymore about my wife. And I mean, I don't care if she just fades away. Moves away. Never shows up at our doorstep ever again. I guess it has to do with finally knowing that it's over.

I'm even getting tired of hearing about it from myself anymore. I have even forgotten what she felt like. Or tasted like. Or even smelled like. Her voice is no longer the sound of someone I knew. If I passed her on the street I think I would just pass her by. It seems to me like she has just blended in with the rest of humanity that I don't know.

Pretty harsh reality to feel at ease with. That is the way, the feeling, I have right now. Have I just found out that now, I don't love her anymore? Yesterday I said, "The only hurtle I have now is a messy house." It can't be this simple can it?

I don't have any bitterness or that much hatred towards her anymore. I don't feel it. It's almost like someone who you've tried to help but didn't do anything to help themselves so you just stop and they fade from your list of people.

I'm going to lie down and try and rest. The banging of cereal bowels and spilled milk will be happening soon. And the yanking out of bed of some sleepy-eyed one that says waa. I couldn't have asked for more.

Day 51

Just a few words as I am going to be busy today. I have found a woman that will come 2 - 3 days a week and clean the house and feed the kids when they come home, that sort of thing. She is a neighbor, a good acquaintance and friend.

She knows what I have been going through with the mom moving out and all that. She and my kids get along really good. There is no fooling around with her romantically so I am not heading that way.

She knows how to get the kids tails working too. And they know that. She is a good organizer too and will help in that too.

I am going out of town today on business with my boss. It's an all day meeting he says. All he said is that I need to look good. So it's the suit time again.

I am doing well in my head. I think in many ways I have grown from child to adult.

Day 52

My boss drove to the meeting which started after coffee and sweets. Got through with the introduction and then the moderator says and we have a special guest today. Called my name, told a story about me fixing a technical problem in a way they hadn't considered, at less cost and less time.

I was given an award and then pictures were taken. After the all day meeting we all went to a steak house for dinner in my honor.

I got home around 11:30 last night. My wife was there. She looked eager and asked me how did it go. What was it about? I told her that they gave me an award. She said it was nice. She left right after that. She said as she was leaving for me to call her if I should ever need anything.

She did wash the dishes and do a load of laundry. That was nice of her.

I have a woman starting next week coming to the house for clean up around 2 or 3 days a week. The kids like her and they respect her because they know she won't take any gaff from them.

Thank God it's Friday. I feel like I just want to stay in bed all weekend.

I did visit my lawyer and he got a one paragraph letter from my wife's lawyer. It simply stated that he, my wife, my lawyer, and me need to get together and work out a solution to the joint custody that she wants and I don't want.

My lawyer said that she like most people don't really know what joint custody really means. I said in my wife's case it means control. Having control over the kids.

So my lawyer called her lawyer to set up a date for all of us to get together. We'll see.

Day 53

My wife's at it again. Calls this morning and says she wants to take my oldest and middle son for the day and night. Will be over in half an hour to pick them up.

The youngest feels left out immediately. And vents that to me. I tell him to ask mommy when she comes over.

She comes over. I am lying in bed because of wanting to give my back a rest this weekend. She comes in closes the door and proceeds to ask me what I am going to do with the kids this summer as far as watching them when they are off. I said that I am not sure at this point but I will make necessary arrangement before then.

She comes back with I don't think its right that you are spending $400 a month to have someone come and clean the house.

When I was here she said I kept the house up and all. You can't do that yourself? And she says she doesn't have a big enough space to bring the kids to. So can I help her out with money to get a house next month she could take the kids to?

I said honey I do not have enough money to maintain two households. She said all I want is some help. I then went on to explain to her that the kids are getting older. Expenses will get higher and that these kids don't even have a savings for their future like college. I want to at least start things like this.

I then got on the soap box. Said you have decided your path and direction in your life. There are consequences for that direction you picked. As well as a direction I have to go myself. The children are number one priority and not you anymore. I cannot and will not get involved with what you have picked for your direction in life. That is your own and you must live with that.

She kept wanting to dart out of the room but would come back when I would start the conversation again.

She said I'm not going to argue about it. I said who's arguing? These are the hard stone facts. She didn't say anything. She went in the other room and very fast left with the two boys.

I am concerned that now she is mad and has the two boys with her. What will she vent on them about me? I have to let the boys have contact and time with their mom but it is these times I wonder what effects this will have on them. Caught in the catch 22 situation.

After the conversation in the room and before she left, she came in and handed me the child support check. Like it was based upon our outcome of the conversation. Talk about manipulation!

How many times does it take now for her to realize that I will not bend in this matter? She chose her path and I will not support her with money anymore.

Now that I am strong and not painfully giving in it seems the shoe is on the other foot. Oh, it affects me. I am shaking right now and keyed up somewhat. I will take a shower and get around. Let this foolishness of hers pass. Waiting for the next round.

I just hope that she doesn't take the kids over to her boyfriend's house. If I find that out I will tell my lawyer again she has done this. We have been tracking and documenting this.

Day 56

I had a wonderful time out with myself Saturday night all the way until Sunday late afternoon. I hated for it to end.

I went to see a blues band. Had a few drinks and danced some. All this made me happy. Not to think about anything at home. My wife watched the kids. She said sure no problem.

When I picked up the kids from her apartment and we were all leaving she said bye boys I love you. And then she said to me see ya, have a nice one. It's interesting that there are two responses or actions as it were. One to the kids and one to me. I am excluded from that part of the feelings she has for the kids.

I stayed overnight at a hotel. It was lonely to say the least. But the time spent out was so great. It gave me a breather which I needed and could feel the difference afterwards.

I asked the kids how their time was over at their mom's. I got a mixed response. I got, ok and ok but not really. My middle son said he doesn't want to go over there because, 1. He's more comfortable at home. 2. Nothing to do over there. 3. No food or at least not the kind he likes or is used to.

I made a good dinner for us last night and watched TV. The kids kept arguing and shuffling their way into who was going to sit close to me. That made me feel wanted. They do this most of the time.

My kids are a life saver and giver. I just give them lots of hugs and time with them. They are not used to having their dad away from them even overnight.

I was thinking this evening it's been close to two years now that my wife has not been around for them. Seeing how the first year was spent working evenings and only seeing their mom on the weekends really. And then the second year close, that she has been moved away from us.

I made it this far and the only thing that I see that needs tightening up on is cosmetic. The house cleaning. And the continued discipline given to the kids for taking responsibilities for their chores and cleaning up. That I think will be a continuing thing.

Tomorrow starts another week. Another set of crises to overcome. Or it can be looked at as a new week of challenges that can be turned into fun in overcoming them. It is all in the way one looks at that glass of water. Half empty or half full.

Day 57

Oldest son was sick today with stomach virus again. I stayed home but he thought I went to work. He called his mom I later found out because around 10am, while dozing on the couch, she came walking in the door.

She went to see son that was sick. Afterwards we were sitting at the kitchen table. We got into a conversation about the pending divorce. I asked her what was her definition of joint custody. What did she really want?

She told me she wants to be able to take the kids to the doctors if anything happens. Being able to be involved with their schooling.

She asked me what I thought what was it worth for the 13 years of marriage. I asked what do you mean? Money? She said she should get help from me in maintaining a portion of the money so she could get a house big enough for the kids and her. Not to pay any child support. She wants the bigger car.

She also said that if I insist with her having to pay child support that she will take the kids away from me. I will live in this house by myself.

I kept having to lower the tone of the conversation because her fangs were showing. She tried to tell me that she was up front telling me about wanting the divorce and not lying about anything. I told her that it is interesting that you do not want to own up to any responsibilities of why and how you went about your exit.

She kept insisting that she did nothing wrong. I told her otherwise. I did tell her that we have to reach an agreement about how we are going to end this marriage that has minimal affect on the kids. She agreed only on her terms.

I don't care if it's joint custody or parenting we end up with as long as this is the kids' domicile.

I told her that I don't like that she is having a relationship with another man throughout all this. She had nothing to say to that. She kept on telling me that she is not and has never been in midlife crisis that it was all my making it up.

I think she was in full blown midlife crisis. She denies it wholeheartedly now and sticks to her guns on that. So

I'm looking at her never coming back. I knew this of course some months ago.

I'm mixed up now in which way to go. Push her into a court battle. Or compromise and have it over with. I cannot see why she should have to not pay anything in child support.

She wants joint parenting. Wants alimony and does not want to pay child support. I should have asked her what she thinks 13 years of marriage is worth for me!

I just don't know. What would be best for the kids. And what would not eat up my income that would just support her?

I have been wrestling with this in my head as how to push for her to pay child support and other responsibilities that come with divorce. Or take her outstretched hand and give her money each month for a house so the kids can have a decent place for them to go visit their mother in. And also a decent neighborhood too.

She sent me an e-mail the other day:

Just thought I'd email a quick note to let you know I'm glad we got together to talk about things that are going on in our mind. I doubt you let me know everything as I didn't open myself fully up to you. I'm glad we realized that we have to work together to make this work out for the kids' sake.

I, like you, go through my periods of anger and there are times when I want to ncil you to the wall with this divorce but what would that dc for me (nothing).

I still can't believe you will not go or haven't gone straight to your lawyer on the things we talked about. I think you have changed and I think you have gotten more conniving as far as getting people to talk just to get information out of them.

I know there is a lot of anger between us but it has nothing to do with the kids. The kids are who we should be thinking of and not what has happened between us and I know you know that. I just want the best for our kids and the best for our kids is us not just you and not just me but us.

That is all I want to say at this time. Thank you again for the talk. I am hoping things can turn out for both of us.

I think her problem is about control. She thinks I controlled her in our marriage. That's what she says. I really can't see that. I have thought and thought about that issue when I was trying to figure out what was wrong about me. That's when I took the trip in finding out about me. I have searched my being as much as possible and I see none of that. It's probably one of perspective maybe? I don't know.

All I do know is that I am not going to go back into that depressive state again that she put upon me and the kids too in a lot of ways. My oldest is screwed up emotionally. My job has suffered because of all this. Even with the award last week.

I am scared that I cannot do all that it will take. That new long candle burned fast and is burning my hands. My health is taking a toll too. I smoke like a chimney.

I think I have to go back into counseling. And my kids need something like that too. Maybe if I don't know what to do, don't!

I am worn down physically. I am tired all the time even when I sleep. I have road maps in my eyes all the time. I put up that happy face to my kids and push along each day.

I hope that all this that I'm going through is worth the jewels and riches that await someone who just tries to do what is right and good. Or will I have to wait till I get to heaven? I need to be smothered in love right now. Someone who genuinely gives me love.

All the kids are over at the neighbor's house swimming in the muddy pond. So it's baths tonight for all of them. Dinner and homework; and some house cleaning too.

Day 58

My wife is constantly bringing every conversation down to money she doesn't have, because she doesn't have a decent job. Well she chose this. I didn't.

So really, I can compromise a little. And that will be that we can have joint custody, I am the primary custodian and she will have to pay child support. That's as far as I'll go. I don't even think she deserves that. She has not changed any. She is calmer now, because her lawyer told her to clean up her act.

She will always be the mother of our children. But I will always be their father too. So let's not forget about me. The one who went the extra thousand miles with her. Gave and gave and gave. Was willing at one time to accept her having an affair so she could get it over with. Boy I was nuts then.

I'm the one who took the bull by the horns and made sure the kids were well as to be expected in their minds and hearts. I listened the many nights and hugged them while they cried. WHY, WHY. Why mommy, did you do this.

I think I am finding my answers myself.

Day 59

When it started, my wife was saying all this stuff about being insecure, not finishing anything in life, not knowing what each day holds. All that stuff.

I felt her pain at that time and was a comforting shoulder to lean on. But she rejected that. Also she led me down many side streets, leading me on with I just want to find myself. Maybe I am in midlife crisis.

I got her into counseling and antidepressants. Bought her a bigger car that she always wanted. Catered to her in every way. Flowers, love poems. Understanding. All.

In the final analysis, it was bullshit she was feeding me. All the while making her escape. She was lying to me but more important was she was lying to herself. Denying and suppressing that which she knew was right. That what she was doing was wrong.

She rationalized everything she was doing. Now she says that she has been truthful with me from the beginning. She in her mind still thinks that she did tell me it was over and wanted a divorce. She has convinced herself to this day still, that she is ok and right in all that she has done since this came out into the open.

She made it a reality by thinking it. She is that convoluted. Coupled with the fact that she destroyed her self-respect and then has suppressed that too and believes it.

So what do I do with a person like that? I think the word is disconnect. She must go away from me. I must go away from her. She will be connected to the family because of the boys. But she will no longer have my sympathies. Nor my support. Emotionally or monetarily. All during this future time I will have to monitor that her actions do not take the children down her road.

I cannot bend in catering to her wants for they are damaging to me and the kids. It is her life and her choices that have defined her. She can't say one thing and do another at her whim. And damn anyone else that gets in her way.

That leads to another thing. Responsibility. Taking ownership of one's actions. She doesn't. The only ownership she has taken so far is what she wants in the now. And that changes every day for her. I and the boys cannot live a life with a crazy person like that.

Day 61

It's Saturday morning with coffee in hand and sun is up but cloudy.

I am feeling much better as far as the back goes. Can't lift anything still and don't want to. The housekeeper which is a neighbor friend has been working on the big clean-up and organization of the house. I gave her the latitude of doing whatever she wants basically with the house. She has done a superb job. I didn't realize how this messiness and the inability to get it cleaned up for some reason had a big affect on my mind.

She and I sat down yesterday evening. And she talked about when she was divorced and a working mom and coming home and taking care of everything. How it was so exasperating that the house could not seem to be in order. She said that it wasn't as hard for her because she just had one child.

She also said that you need to start with a clean slate as far as the house goes and that's what she wants to provide me with. The kids love me and mind me. And respect me.

The kids all gave her a hug before she left. Even me. She is a great strong neighbor that realizes I need help. And is stepping up to the bat.

My wife is paying child support on time each month doing this now due to the temp court order. I just hate confrontations. I did find out that her mom and dad apparently will give her money if she needs for a house. But will not apparently keep it up for her. So I think things might get nasty within the next month.

Day 63

Whenever I can get an emotionally industrious talk with my wife I do it. But have learned to not expect anything.

My wife and I had a long talk this morning. I did most of the talking at first. Then I said I have been talking too much. It's your turn.

She opened up with I taught my kids wrong. I did everything for them while they were young. And later I expected them to do what I have been doing for them. Cleaning. taking care of one's self. Hollering didn't help. No respect from the kids. It was all my fault that they are like they are. She said that I was not the fault. This house represents a failure to me.

I talked to her about my times in the past of just coming home and plopping down in front of the tube and then eating and doing the same. That something was happening in my life then that I did a lot to not think about problems. Mine was TV, eat, sex.

I told her that while she was gone I had a lot of time to evaluate myself and to look critically at myself and then doing something about it. Mainly what I found out. Learned that love is not only physical but more of a reading of your spouse's wants. Being that close to be supportive in helping her.

Getting the kids into where they want to do chores and such. The respect, from out of love. My kids don't exhibit that. Our kids love us deeply. They just won't do anything. I have found out from the close to two years of me raising them on my own dealing with all the details.

I ended with please give this thought, if you want to take the chance again with me and the boys. I drove that home many times. We stood there in the hot sun facing each other. I said again, honey, think about what we talked about. Please give me some kind of sign. She smiled and nodded. We embraced and we kissed. Said goodbye and hugged again.

So it's that time again to move that inch that she seems to move, every time we have in-depth conversations like this. It is those times that progress seems to be made. This process is way too slow of course. For most people.

Her actions now will decide the outcome.

I asked her about the other man and she said smiling, he feeds me. Gives me gas for the car sometimes. I swelled my chest and said you know I want to do that. She said that she has to humble herself when those times came to ask for money. After all, she said, I told you that I was going to move out and see if I could support myself. Do it on my own.

So this is a mixture of marriage, drifting apart thing, and of midlife. Which, think in our case was a brew for crisis.

Time will tell and if I don't receive any response at all I'll know that my words didn't mean anything to her. For they are true and from the heart.

Day 64

I got a phone call from my lawyer today. She and I and the lawyers will meet together this Friday afternoon. They will apparently outline what she wants from the divorce.

I didn't hear from my wife today like I kind of expected after the talk we had. I think it's probably gone sour. It will probably be the same old bla bla bla. Again.

The only real turn with actions that I will truly believe is that she severs and ends all with her boyfriend. And tells me about it.

Even if she says she wants to stay away for a while longer I could accept that. But not with jumping into bed with men. That's the killer there for me.

If anyone really cares about another spouse and all the heart to heart felt talks we have had, still continues, doesn't have my support anymore in any which way.

She knows it's her choice and what she will have to live with. And she picks it anyways. She must feel pretty bad about herself to choose a life without her kids and I. I know me and what I am capable of in relationships and love and all that entails. I do have good qualities and compassion and love that woman seeks.

I'm not stuck on myself either. I have grown into a man. A good man. And she knows it. She laughs about it all. Makes jokes about it sometimes.

I don't have any more to say that I haven't said already. I have exhausted everything. So it's still her problem. And that's it. I'm moving on.

Will I take that chance again with her in engaging in heartfelt conversations? I don't know. It will be up to her. Actions honey. Actions. And they better be sincere!!!!

Day 66

Wife calls tonight and says why don't we have my oldest son's birthday on Saturday, which she said earlier. I say why don't we have it on Sunday? That way we can celebrate both at the same time. Mother's Day and his birthday.

Later while checking e-mails, one is from wife. Says that we don't have to celebrate Mother's Day. She said she really doesn't need one.

So screw her. I'm having one on Saturday just like it was planned.

I'm getting pretty ticked off about all this. I really am! I'm ready not to give her any avenues of chances anymore. She didn't deserve any that I gave her before. Over and over and over again. With love, compassion, and forgiveness attached to all.

She has until and during Friday when we all get together with the lawyers to give me a sign. And she knows it. I will come down so hard on her that she will never want to see me again. And that's where I will want it.

I will sell this house later and move away with the kids. I don't see her coming around and that's her choice and loss. For her loss will be so great that her life will be forever tormented with guilt in those important hours of her sleep. When she sees all around her laughing children, she will cry in anguish for the rest of her life.

I know that she is their mother and always will be. But she "can" be replaced. Better than the constant pain she is putting them through now. They will be happy. I will make sure of that.

I tried to be the Mr. civil guy. The Mr. "its ok, you can have your life and Oh its hunky dorey" to her. Hell it's been a year and a half. She can laugh herself to her grave.

I know now what is really, really important. Me and my welfare in mind body and spirit. And my kids' most of all. She doesn't even enter the picture anymore. For anything. Hell she doesn't even deserve the printed space I am using here!!!

I know that after she is gone and my healing mind and heart mends there will be a woman out there who would appreciate a man like me.

I am so happy that my good qualities which make me a good person were not destroyed by a soul bond love that's been torn from the flesh of my heart.

This is a glimpse of the importance I place upon matrimony, vows, placing that which is me in the hands of another. And I'm not talking about co-addiction. I'm talking about the bonds of love that grow and grow to where if there is a severance, a death happens within both.

But with our marriage it is only me. I won't make that mistake again. Of course I will do it again. With someone else. Love is that way.

I just made my rounds checking on the boys sleeping. It makes it all worthwhile when you stare into the beautiful sleeping faces of your children.

I thought of taking my wedding band to a secluded lake with guitar and bottle in hand and then tossing it out into the lake. Or I will wear it on court day. Then take it off and toss it to that lady.

I know this entry is long but to have no one to share my anguished pissed off thoughts to. At least I'm not in deep depression like this would have put me into a while back. I knew what I was getting into when I approached her again with heart to hearts. For one thing I will know more of how deeply she is away from us. I am a person that gives chances to the nth degree.

Life is what I make it. I don't have to accept any of this kind of treatment from my wife. I accepted in the past because I cared about her so much. But now I don't and that is her problem. Because once I let go of that, that caring and compassion and love, she will be forever forgotten. I won't look over my shoulder. I will place many walls up in our relationship that she will be a non person to me.

I won't be deceiving or conniving. I will explain the boundaries flat out and stick to them. I felt like saying to her, that every time she is in bed with her boyfriend having sex that she think of me. She doesn't deserve to feel good.

Day 67

Time to be a man. I am a man that has lost his perspective. Lost himself in the life of another. My wife. It was a conscious decision many times to get lost in her with the problems I thought I could somehow help her with.

I found out that she thinks that nothing is wrong. And this is just a path that is normal these days.

It's ok to squeeze the life out of someone that is trying to help and then defecate on them.

Well today she died. In my mind that is. And my heart and soul. I let her go today. I am not normal she says. Everyone else that goes through this just quits and goes on. There is something wrong with me.

We had the powwow with our lawyers today. Nothing really got accomplished other than they are going to write up a proposal and forward it to my lawyer then me.

My lawyer said in cases like this to where both people are acting like adults, it will turn out ok. He said he not only represents the adults but the children.

All I have to say is that she is dead to me. I have no buttons for her to push anymore. I am free now to go on about my life.

The grieving has been done now. That's what I've been doing I think in my mind. Knowing. But not facing. I've faced death many times and have resolved myself to that and charged forward. But this facing is a death face with a name and experiences attached to it.

So I throw out words that impale themselves onto my wife's deaf ears and mind. I am not a joke and my love and the reality of my passions are not a joke. Those are real and tangible feelings that can be felt and are felt by others. Touching others without touching.

Today's encounter with my wife's inability for feeling real love stuck me. Her chord was out of tune with my resonant chord. I no longer want her because she is not the type of person I want.

We are just going through the worldly legal issues because we have children. My children, our children deserve, no, demand from us the responsibility of goodness and upbringing and of moral qualities that are Judeo-Christian virtues.

She has told by her action and I told her so, that living with another man and then taking our children over there introducing them to him is teaching them that it is ok to be married and go out and have another person as such like a married person.

I don't know. I guess I will continue this slow movement with my life to get her out of my system. I can't seem to speed it up other than taking the destructive route. And that would be to be the disgruntled and bitter hatred person. But I don't want to end up like that. So goodness waits on those that suffer and come to understanding about themselves. And that statement is a book unto itself.

Am I a man? Today I took the first step. I think.

Day 76

It's been a while since I have felt like writing about my life. Time to play catch-up.

I have been getting back into work since the back surgery and have gone on some dates. It was interesting the one girl that I was hanging around with for a while. Last weekend as usual she and I drove around the city and went to flea markets and such.

In the evening she drove us around. All the while talking about and ranting and raving about her husband that locked her out for the past three months for the second time.

She drove past his home and then some bars where he hung out. Then it happened. She spotted his car at a bar. I told her to stop. After she explained what he looked like I went in ordered a beer and looked around. Talked to one man there and went out and said I didn't see him. Then she and I went in. She indicated her husband. It was the man I struck up a conversation with.

She went to the bar and I re-introduced myself to her husband. He now knew we were together. He was cordial as well as I.

We sat there for well over an hour just talking about different things in life interspersed with their marriage problems. He was open and I was open with our talking.

The bar closed and that was the night. She and I talked well into the night and watched the sun come up. Went to her daughter's house and had coffee and donuts.

I went home and started the work week. This Friday I call and talk with her daughter. She says that I don't know what you talked about to her husband but "Mom" hasn't been home for two days. She is back with husband. They have been talking and she doesn't know what is up.

I haven't talked to her since but am glad and happy that they are together. I hope for the best for the both of them. I naturally will not see her anymore. It wouldn't be right. I understand a man's feelings in this regard. Let it lie.

So there is sunshine in life. Happiness for lost souls out there.

What's really happening inside my life? Coming to closure that my wife is never coming back. Moving on with knowing of that in my heart. Finally having rest with that.

I do have my times though. Like today when I find out that her parents that were like a mom and dad to me are coming to visit for a weekend. They will not come here. They will see her and stay at a hotel. That hurts. Another thing I have no control over so must let that go.

I think that many things I will have to let go concerning her side of the family and that I will end up because of these circumstances, a totally new life built by myself. Like anything new it is frightening and scary not knowing if I will make the right choices and do the right things.

My boys and I and life ticks on and on. Each day I grow older and the carving of I love you on the tree gets weathered. I feel like in the movie, "The Ghost and Mrs. Muir." The carving on the beach post and as years go by it is weathered by the waves and winds of time. I wait for that ghost... could it be that floating soul that was lost? The real wife that I knew, and loved, and cherished?

Of course in reality there is a woman out there for me. To keep the spontaneity and spice of life which I have not lost. I know myself and the qualities I have and hold dear. I am a giver. Not a taker. I do take from life but not at the hurting expense of others.

What tomorrow holds? I don't know. But I do know that I can face the world knowing that love WILL rule in the end. So there I stand with each sunset and each sunrise reaffirming myself. I get some of that back too by the people I bump into on my days trek.

Through all this with my wife, I have done a lot with trying to help her. When it became so bad with her and her boyfriend, getting beat up, her family not wanting anything to do with me anymore. Her flinging hatred. I finally disconnected with her. Went for a divorce which she wanted.

Now her being faced with having nothing, she is fighting for everything moneywise. She doesn't deserve anything. She walked out the door into the arms that night with the other man.

Should I keep a friendly, cordial relationship with my wife? I know actions speak louder than words. She invited me to a family day at her work this weekend of fun and games for the kids and all. What did I do? I gave it right back to her. The way she many times did it to me. I smiled at her and shook my head no. That was it. That's the way she always answered me when I tried to invite her with family things to do together.

I don't talk to her. Can't trust her. Is giving her back the same she does to me good?

A twinge of light is in the sky. I think I'll watch another sunrise.

I'll close on that positive note.

Day 77

I think I am going to refocus on building a new life. I am sure ready and deserve a better one. How to do all the particulars, I have no idea. But a start is a must.

On a lighter note. It is 6am Monday morning and the kids are in the tub. They went swimming in a muddy pond yesterday and didn't get their baths. Three days of school left before their summer vacation.

Clothes are in the dryer and minutes a ticking away before the bus comes. Countdown to seconds around here. That's how close we make it.

Youngest kid refuses to use soap so it is up to me to rough up his pores with the sweet stuff.

Day 78

This where I put effort on a new life. Maybe at first half heartedly but I know I must, in a movement towards an unknown.

I will approach it as only I can with wisdom I gathered from the guts of knowing and actions that others are depending on me. Look up to me. The horrid stares of, will it be ok. Will we make it out of here? I take some of that but not all during my first inroads on this new life I must make. For I travel with flesh and blood of my sons.

At this time, I am at a road looking forward. Scanning the terrain. One road/path with jungles of brush, inviting possibly an ambush. Another with wide open area that would if we were there, would have no place for cover. To set up camp maybe and fortify the perimeter and stay is another option. But one with constant vigilance.

This is the time in my life where I must make decisions that will affect the outcome of not only myself but everyone connected. For from death there is rebirth. A changing.

The death of my nation, even so small as my family has great implications for generations to come. These are the questions that plague my mind as I contemplate my new movement towards a new life.

So this is just a start and a beginning. A thought. A plan. A frightening one as one in command. Hurt. Someone, something will get hurt. Maybe die to emerge into something else.

Love, compassion. desire for qualities that are God given. Understood by the heavens and given by the spark from the hand of God's wisdom is all I can pray for.

So I lift my glass of bitters with the crown seal etched. God save the Queen. God save us all.

Looking back over my shoulder, seeing how far I've gone, I never thought that this would be such a work out. I feel I am ready. All of my life maybe it has been working up to this point. I don't know. It is again me and my mind walking through the boulders and pebbles of life.

I came to my heart and asked, are you broken? For the rest of me hurts. I feel disjointed and ask for your help healing my hurts. There seemed to be a long pause.

A picking of feeling words from my heart. The silence was broken by a scream of cries with tears and feelings all coming at once. Making no sense but of brokenness. The rest of me cries. Finally. Breaking down with sobs and blubbering.

I have made all my last appeals. A small voice keeps repeating. Deep within my soul. I have to keep telling myself, I don't love her anymore. Love. It is a plague of life. Of relationships. One I choose to have forever in my life. Count me in on that.

One thing I need is to pick one thing I like to do. To get into that and give it my all. Give it the intensity and fervor I have always given life. My life is half full. Not half over.

Here! Meet someone that is full of vigor where time and life never ends. The dance of life and all that is good never ends. To feel the lips close to mine and the passion of forever is mine.

I throw this out to the world. My words. My life. As it is and forever was. I am not cut from a regular mold.

I no longer request a better life. I demand it. I punctuate it with exclamation points wherever and whenever I can. Every word and action is clung to and given its reward.

I am not perfect. Far from it and thank God. For there is more that meets the eye as far as marriage and the troubles that hide within.

Baby, close that suitcase that you been packing. Let's all unpack. Unpack our lives. What was once one, let it be again. But it is different. A new beginning. Each separately but together. Those are what we are dealing with now.

Are we dealing with our significant other or with ourselves? We all arrive at our own answers or so we think. It is ok. We cannot control the actions of others. Even when they are our fathers or mothers.

We can only cross those loosely or bonded ridged bridges with lives known of our selves. Knowing ourselves. So what journey are we on? When all shit breaks open.

Ok now I have kids. What do I do with them during my travels though this loss and transition of wife. Lost to the wind? Changing my life. A new beginning. They have an education that is needed. Can they get it from my wanting to get a 45 ft catch, live aboard and sail the world?

Can I, will I, fill my glass and be buried and leave my children to fend for a life that will afford them a quality life? Or should I wait for the afterlife? God will provide. Oh so many questions and no answers. Only the outcome from actions.

All this that I am going through is twofold. A midlife crisis or transition folded onto my life. The folds in my life were always transitions. Sometimes immediate due to nicety. For we take what comes. React.

I am clogged with disjointed thoughts of what and how to do progress with my life. Children. I will always do what is right by them. Give up my dreams even. For I am responsible. Always will be to them.

Day 80

When love and help arrive it arrives with spontaneity. At least that's what happened today. The yard has grown into a mess of weeds because I haven't been able to do anything for some time as a result of my back surgery.

My neighbor came over today while I was at work with a mower and weed eater and everything and did all the stuff to make the yard look good. It was a total surprise. I feel uplifted and that is just what I needed. Someone who cared enough to show it by doing something with actions.

They are nice people that work hard for what they have. They have two kids. They play with my kids all the time.

Contrast this with my wife who is taking care of the kids during the day for summer vacation. She came, got the kids, and went over to her one room apartment and that's where they stayed most of the day.

I asked them if they cte lunch and they said no. She left them at my house and went to her job at three. Nothing was done in the house. Not a dish. Nada.

White. Black. Day. Night. That's the difference with someone who really cares and someone who doesn't.

I don't want to write about her anymore. She is not worth it. Even with my back healing this help today made my healing much better.

I know I will come out of this a much better man.

Day 81

It's Friday evening and the lights are coming on quickly for this holiday weekend. The steaks are on the grill, probably burning by now. The wife is taking the kids Saturday am and will have them back Sunday am. I plan on using that short time to fill it with mad dashes at some sort of happiness.

What will I do? Visit or try to find a neighbor friend and his family and take a bed roll at the state park. I hope I find them. If not I will deluge myself with favorite foods and whiskey. And beer. Think about this holiday and my personal thoughts of being thankful that I am here and not in some rotted hole in some foreign land and forgotten.

I could have been there a few times, knowing that heart pounding fright. We all have our darkest moments. I will probably visit the local cemetery and read the tombstones. Say a few prayers to ones that I don't know.

This is the start of my memorial weekend.

Day 82

It is Saturday night and my son and I are together tonight and we are all spiffed up and going out for pizza and to play video games. I will even wear my sunglasses indoors. Cool

We all think. We all have ideas. Some we react to and put them into motion. Some we do not. I find myself putting most into actions. I have a feeling I am going to end up being the way out extroverted guy.

A bum on the street in a cardboard box. I can sit with him and have a decent conversation. The doctor or physicist I can hold a conversation. Have them waiting for the punch line. You know what? I am better off without her. I said before that she held me back by me wanting to help her.

I was the one denied fullness. I just wanted her to realize and come along with me, I guess. Well it doesn't matter now. I know what I want.

Life will be ok and here comes my son burping like a true man. Says we have to go.

Day 83

My oldest and I went out last night. I let him drive the back road up to the main road. He did very well. It was wonderful to sit there in the passenger seat and listen to him talk and talk and drive. He performed perfect to oncoming cars going the other way on the country road. It was night time too.

We stayed out till about 10:30 and went home. We drove up to the house and parked, went in, and all of a sudden my middle son comes out of the darkness. Then I see taillights going up the road. My wife's car. She was parked down the road, lights off waiting for us.

I then ask him what's going on? He basically tells me, it's boring with mommy. Nothing to do. So we all get into the house. I put on the movie Signs. Cheese, dip, potato chips and beer. Late into the night we watch this scary movie. Needless to say, we all fell asleep together in front of the TV.

I don't quite know how to analyze all this. I just know I don't like this up and down that the kids are being pulled into. They seem alright. But?

Soon her car will drive up to drop off the littlest one. She can then go to her honey's house and spend time with that family that's not threatening to her I guess. I have a feeling she is going to lose the kids. Not legally. They will drift from her. And she, I believe, will run away from them like she has with me.

So I must prepare for that time if and when it comes. All I know is that I am ok emotionally most of the time. Stable with a few frightening details of the divorce that I screwed up on. Financial paperwork that I didn't get done and they want it. I also need to scrape up more money for my lawyer. Oh well. Tra la la, life goes on.

I am sure that what ever happens in the end I will be ok and damn the torpedoes, the kids will be happy once again! My wife says to me that she cannot come to our home because it reminds her of failure. I feel for her in that respect. I have empathy. But all the other baggage and crap she continues to do living with her boyfriend and thinking I don't know what she is really up to.

I know more about her than she thinks. I cannot fix her. She has to fix herself. She is broken somehow in this time of her life. I tried but there comes a time where decisions have to be made for one's own survival. And in my case there are also three little souls along with that.

I can only lead by example, love, outward love and affections. They know that. They also know my hurt in their own way.

They come to me spontaneously and hug and say "I love you daddy." Oh! talk about out of the mouths of babes. This is strength drawn from them also just by that action.

I don't hang onto the old anymore. I take one day at a time and try to think of it as the last day.

My wife drove up and sat in her car. I saw her forlorn eyes that I in my analysis feel say she had a bad night last night. My son abandoning her, or some such thing. I just saw it in her eyes. She didn't look at me.

The little one bumbled into the house and she drove off. For her days of what I will not know. Empathy for her I feel. Interrupting her life with my talking and my thoughts on this matter is no longer happening. I used to do that. It is her life now. What and how she travels it is her choice.

Me? I deluge my life with keeping close to the action of her existence sometimes. Just to be close to the edge. Close to the waters. I step on the rocks in that river while my wife is the stream. Sometimes I misstep and plunge my foot into her stream. Is that so bad?

I live close to the edge. Always have. The excitement of such is the exhilarating knowledge I glean from peoples' lives regardless of who or where or what. As well as my personal life with my family.

We are going to clean up the house and get our day going. It is with assertive spontaneity that I will be going out this late afternoon with the kids on a trek to the lake, taking 1/4 lb hot dogs and charcoal and grill and hamburger patties with all the fixings.

We are striking out not knowing the day's outcome but will always give and enlist happiness where ever we go. The kids want to get out so this is it.

Day 84

I have a few moments this morning to catch up about yesterday's trek. We had a good time at the lake. My favorite place right by the cliff was open. We set everything up and the kids went swimming right away.

I sat watching them from the cliff. Splashing and frolicking in the water. I popped a top and played guitar watching the sun's dancing on the water.

It didn't hurt so bad watching the families around the campgrounds with some cuddling and laughing. Sometimes with kids, one doesn't even get out of the drive yet, when the kids are all yelling and kicking and making a disturbance.

I stopped with all the noise and I looked up to my left outside the car. My eyes found a tree so close you could touch it with its deep green lush leaves bending and twisting in the breeze. It was like it was looking back at me, waving with its leaves. At that moment I didn't hear anything but silence. And it felt good.

The silence was broken by the kids saying, are we going? I looked back in the car and said are you ready? A resounding YES! On our way it was not as noisy.

While I was sitting and watching the lake, the boys came running back all cold and wanting a fire started. We had forgotten towels. They went out searching for wood and soon we had a big fire going. Now it was them playing with the fire.

I fired up the grill and made hotdogs and hamburgers and cooked a steak. We sat and ate. The sun was sinking and the sky beheld a golden yellow and browns. It was my time now to sit with guitar and sing as the sun set. For this is all I wanted to do.

Day 85

Yesterday was a good day. Didn't start out very well. I have been still working on the kids and their stubborn insistence of not helping out in a way to make this house work.

Cleaning. I still have to prod them along and seemingly direct their every move in cleaning. They know how to clean. They just do the minimal.

Well early evening, I invited the neighbors over for dinner. Two racks of ribs with all the fixings. We all ate. Did the dishes and sat outside on the patio. Since there were six young ones a baseball game began and ended up being a whole lot of fun.

The little ones against the big ones. The little ones won with the help of us grown ups of course. But there was none of this bickering among the kids that normally there is. It was nice to end the day like that.

It is now work day. I plan on taking today off for making appointments and running around that I have put off. Got a leak somewhere in the bathroom that I can't seem to isolate.

How am "I" doing. Really? I am holding on to that feeling of "it will be ok in the end." I can't wait till this divorce thing is all over. A sigh of relief I believe will happen. Also some sorrow that will and must be dealt with. At least I know it's coming.

My job is there. My house is intact. I move more now than one day at a time. I don't collapse and roll up into a ball with excruciating pain of what's been dealt in my life.

Day 89

My wife and soon to be ex whatever which way it goes will happen next Friday. She told me over the phone the other day that she is taking a day job where she works at now. She had two other chances before when we were together trying to work things out.

Now that summer has hit and the kids are out of school she decides to do this. Why??? It is because of spending time with her boyfriend, that's why.

The other reason is that it takes too much work to be with the children all day for her.

So with one night's notice I scramble to provide an adult chaperone for my kids.

My wife had said that we could send one of the kids to her sister's and one to her other sister and another to her mom and dad's.

I immediately told her no. I will have someone watching them and taking care of them. She wanted to know who. I said I have someone in mind. I didn't but I thrive on crisis management and do a good job at it.

Tonight I invited my neighbor and her husband out to eat with us at a Mexican place. Naturally the two youngest wanted corn dogs. We the grown ups had margaritas. Several in fact. We had a good time.

I am at a crossroads here in my life. I have to make a new life for myself. Positioning myself around positive happy people is a good start I think. Me, not knowing what and how to go about starting over, all I know that it is something I need and must do. I cannot live alone within my self realities.

Gingerly touching others now and feeling the countenance of others. I am a ball of clay in many ways and don't quite know what touches there must be to form what is me.

My wife has done her dirty little deed shoveling more dirt on the grave of our marriage and now on our friendship that I thought we would need to hold our kids together.

I have nothing to shovel now for my life is so new and blemishes are not known or seen. For all is new.

I struggle alone now.

I just love that woman laying in the sunshine. She is mine and I will someday meet her and there will be two.

First of all, I must make a list. Start on things visual. Like a clean inside car. A clean bedroom. Trading those times of just sitting around, for doing something constructive around the house.

I think one of the reasons my kids are not doing anything to help is their frustration maybe at their feelings that they have lost their mother.

How does one counteract that? Reach a point at which to bring them back to a feeling that they have not lost anything? They are young and don't understand. Or they do but don't know how to handle it.

These are some of the challenges I face at this time. The marriage is all over. She has chosen her life. Now I am faced with not reacting to this, her choices anymore. But more so of me living my life the way it was meant to be. It is now with three young boys, not as before when I was just me, single.

I am the same loving, caring, compassionate person that I've always been. I am so glad I have not lost any of the good qualities which are me.

God provides for me. Like the other day. A check came in the mail from the dealer I bought the car from. It was a refund from life insurance. I needed that and was wondering where I would get extra money because of all the time I had to take off because of my back surgery and low paychecks I was getting.

Today is the first day of the rest of my life. I've said it before but now it rings with much more meaning.

There has been so much turmoil but there is a wagon train leaving for a place where a new life will begin and happier trails along the way.

The sun will still beat down and burn us sometimes. And the jagged hills and snowy mountain passes we all have to traverse will still be there.

But we will arrive at that peak and look down at the green rolling valleys and the oceans beyond knowing that it was all worth it and will have grown so much in our lives that when that face of another, you will see and fall in love with, will mean that much more than before.

I believe true love is loving yourself first.

I did not intentionally want to write of these things. But I am learning to get out of me onto paper and voice the inner feelings and thoughts I have always held dear.

We are the winners in our lives when we apply those truths within us and deal with them.

Some put to rest.

Some a life long struggle.

But knowing them is an answer unto itself.

Pat Gaudette is an author, publisher, and website developer. She is the author of several books including:

How to Survive Your Husband's Midlife Crisis: Strategies and Stories From the Midlife Wives Club

Journaling through His Midlife Crisis: Redefining Your Life As He Reinvents His

Teen Mom: A Journal

How to Be a Self-Published Author: A Step-by-Step Guide

Advice for an Imperfect Single World

Advice for an Imperfect Married World

Midnight Confessions: True Stories of Adultery

Sparky the AIBO: Robot Dogs & Other Robotic Pets

Ugly Dolls the Naber Kids Story

She is the founder/webmaster of popular relationship-oriented websites including *The Midlife Club* (MidlifeClub.com) and the award-winning *Friends and Lovers the Relationships Guide* (FriendsandLovers.com). She and her husband live in Florida.

Email her at: pat@patg.com

Visit her website: www.patg.com

How to Survive Your Husband's Midlife Crisis:
Strategies and Stories from The Midlife Wives Club

Authors: Pat Gaudette & Gay Courter

Home & Leisure Publishing, Inc.

ISBN 978-0-9825617-5-1

Available in Paperback, Kindle

& eBook Versions

You've heard all the jokes about men's midlife crises – the new sports car, the new exercise regimen... and the new girlfriend. But when you're the wife trying to cope, it's no laughing matter.

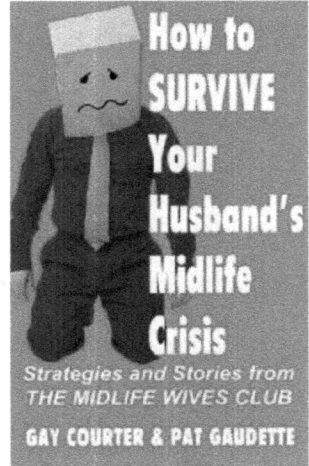

A midlife crisis can devour a relationship. It may be devouring yours. In this guide, you'll find wisdom from both midlife wives and experts on:

- Recognizing *the symptoms*
- Coping *with the threat (or reality) of infidelity*
- Identifying *underlying problems like depression and anger*
- Deciding *when to stick it out – and when to pack it in*
- Protecting *your kids from the fallout*
- Making it through the crisis... *and coming out stronger, saner, and more self-reliant*

With personal stories from real women (and men) and a comprehensive list of resources, **How to Survive Your Husband's Midlife Crisis** *can help you get past the rough spots – and turn this tumultuous time into a change for the better.*

Available in paperback as well as eBook and Kindle versions through Amazon.com and other retailers. For immediate support for midlife issues visit www.MidlifeClub.com.

Teen Mom: A Journal

Edited by: Pat Gaudette
Home & Leisure Publishing, Inc.
ISBN 978-0-9761210-8-4
Available in Paperback, Kindle
& eBook Versions

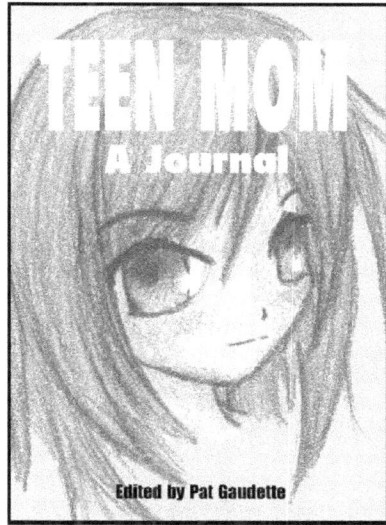

Sixteen-year-old "Katie" was half way through her junior year of high school when she became pregnant. Throughout her pregnancy and for several months afterward, she kept a journal. This is her story as told in that journal.

Katie is not one teenager dealing with unplanned pregnancy, she is one of many. She may be the girl next door or the girl in the next block. She may be your daughter. She may be you.

Teens are more openly sexually active than in past generations and unplanned pregnancy is not the social stigma of years ago. The pregnancy of pop idol Britney Spears' 16-year-old sister, actress Jamie Lynn Spears, was good fodder for the media but it didn't cause her to lose a starring role in Zoey 101, *a television show drawing a large viewership aged 9-14. When vice-presidential candidate Sarah Palin announced her 17-year-old daughter, Bristol, was five months pregnant, it gave teen pregnancy even more of a stamp of "normalcy."*

What is it like to be a pregnant teen? Let teen mom Katie tell you about it. She is one of more than half a million teens facing unplanned pregnancies each year according to data from The National Campaign to Prevent Teen and Unplanned Pregnancy.

Available in bookstores and online through Amazon.com and other retailers.

Midnight Confessions:
True Stories of Adultery

Author: Pat Gaudette

Home & Leisure Publishing, Inc.

ISBN 978-09761210-4-6

Available in Paperback, Kindle

& eBook Versions

Midnight Confessions

TRUE STORIES OF ADULTERY

Pat Gaudette

Why does a person cheat? What type of person cheats? What type of person loves a cheat? Can adultery be forgiven? Can a marriage survive the adultery of one or both partners? Can a cheater be trusted not to cheat again?

Love and lust are powerful forces but with enough time and tears each of us comes to a point of decision making when faced with betrayal.

If you are the betrayed spouse, do you confront? Do you leave? Do you get revenge by cheating? If you are the betrayer, do you lie or tell the truth? Do you keep the affair going or end it to save your marriage? If you are the other person, do you accept what you can get or do you force confrontation to "get it all"?

Midnight Confessions: True Stories of Adultery *examines adultery from the adulterer's point of view, as well as that of the betrayed spouse and the other person. These are their stories in their words. Perhaps after reading their stories and the thought-provoking discussions in this book you will have a better understanding of the decision you need to make to fit your situation.*

Available in bookstores and online through Amazon.com and other retailers.

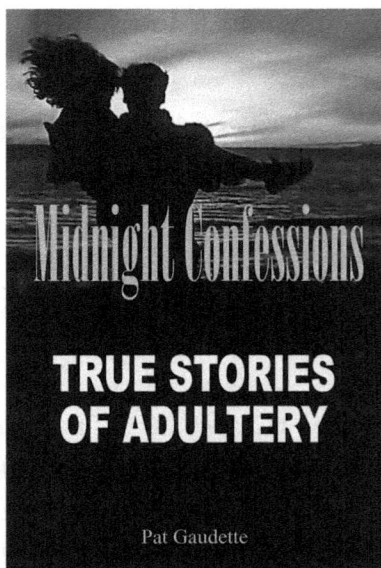

Advice for an Imperfect Single World

ISBN 978-09761210-0-8

Advice for an Imperfect Married World

ISBN 978-09761210-2-2

Available in Paperback, Kindle & eBook Versions

The outspoken "Queen of Hearts" is rarely without an opinion and since 1996 she has been sharing her thoughts about relationships in her advice column for the Friends and Lovers *Web site.* Advice for an Imperfect Married World *focuses on situations facing married couples and couples involved in long term relationships.* Advice for an Imperfect Single World, *focuses on dating issues.*

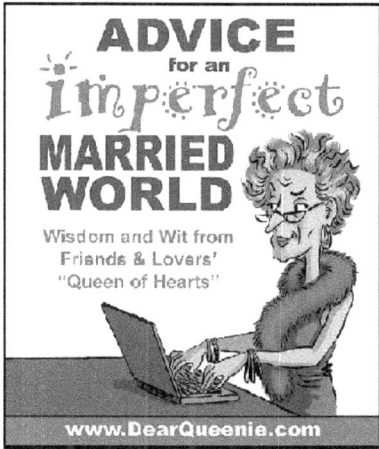

"Dear Queenie, me and my wife have split up and now we're trying to get back but she wants to be friends and take it slow. I'm afraid that we will just be friends and that's all. I want to know if we can be good friends and still be husband and wife and how can I show her that I want both?" - *Peter.*

"Peter, what you're really asking is how do you fast forward through all the friendship stuff and get right down to having sex again. While sex may be your top priority, developing a strong friendship is hers. If you are serious about wanting to repair your marriage you'll put your sex drive on hold and work on the friendship for now." - *Queenie*